I0797283

Little People, **BIG DREAMS**™

BEATRIX POTTER

Written by
Maria Isabel Sánchez Vegara

Illustrated by
Sara Rhys

**Frances Lincoln
Children's Books**

In a lovely part of London called South Kensington, there lived a very curious child. Her parents named her Helen, but she became known by her middle name: Beatrix. She felt a deep love for animals, trees, and everything in nature.

Beatrix didn't go to school. She learned at home with a teacher, and her only friends were her little brother, Bertram, and their many pets. They had mice, fluffy rabbits, bats, and even a prickly hedgehog! She loved drawing them all.

Her parents soon noticed Beatrix had an irresistible desire to draw everything, from the birds in a book to the insects she saw at the museum.

She also kept a diary. It was written in a secret code only she could understand.

Each summer, Beatrix spent her vacation in the countryside in Scotland, and later in England's Lake District—a place so beautiful, it looked like it came straight out of a story book. Beatrix hoped it would stay that way forever . . .

After years of art lessons, Beatrix started earning a little money with her drawings. Some became Christmas cards, and others were used in books of poems and stories. She dreamed that one day, she'd make a book of her own.

Then, while on vacation, Beatrix sent a letter to her little friend Noel. In it, she wrote and drew a made-up story about her rabbit, Peter. It was funny and just a tiny bit scary. Noel loved it so much that Beatrix decided to turn it into a book.

The Tale of Peter Rabbit followed a naughty little rabbit who sneaked into Mr. McGregor's garden after his mom told him not to. Beatrix made him feel so real that he leaped off the page, right into everyone's hearts!

She believed in her story so much that she paid for it to be printed. People loved it! The next year, a company offered to publish it for her and printed many more copies. That was the start of her life as a children's writer and illustrator.

Beatrix had another great idea—what if kids could play with Peter Rabbit, not just read about him? She made a doll that looked like him. She also created games, wallpaper, and tea sets using her book characters, in a way that was totally new.

She used the money she made to buy a farm in the Lake District. Later, Beatrix married William, a kind man who also loved nature.

Together, they worked on the land and helped protect the hills, fields, and sheep around them.

Yet she never stopped writing! Beatrix made more than twenty books filled with exciting adventures, beautiful drawings, and unforgettable characters. Later, her stories even came to life in cartoons and movies.

WELCOME
TO
HILL TOP

She gave much of her land and farms to the National Trust, a group that takes care of special places in the United Kingdom. Thanks to her, the countryside that inspired her stories has been kept safe for everyone to enjoy.

And still today, little Beatrix and all her furry, feathery, and froggy friends bring joy to children everywhere, reminding us that even the smallest creatures have a story to tell.

BEATRIX POTTER

(Born 1866 – Died 1943)

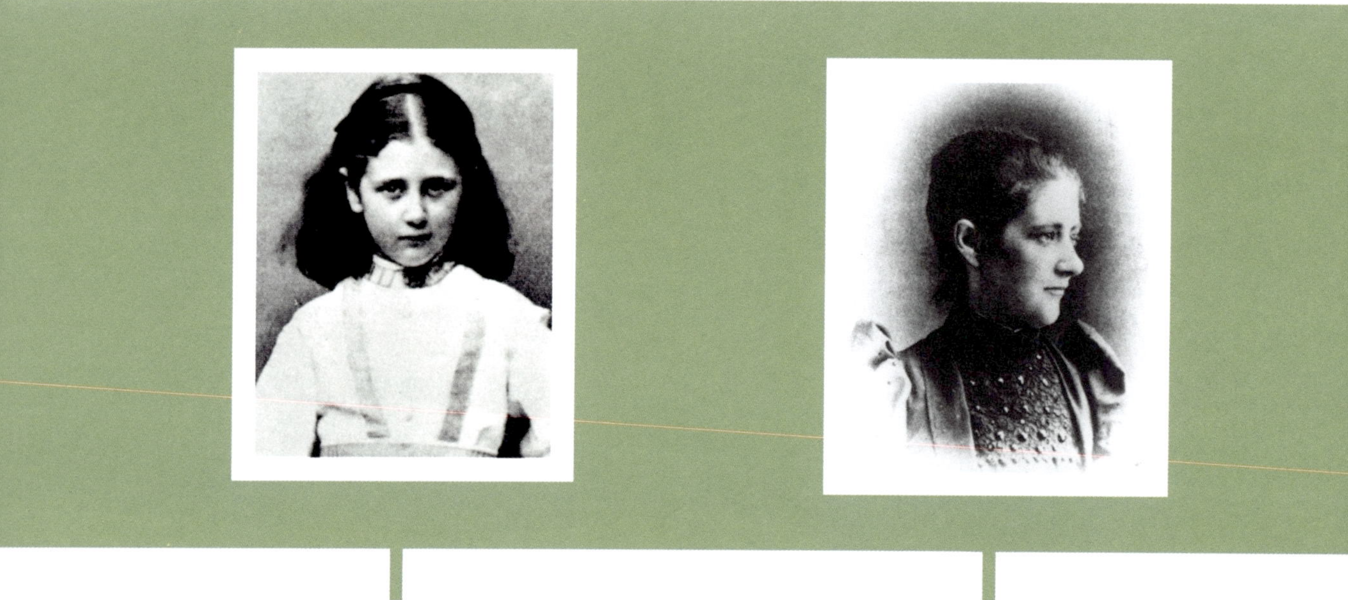

c. 1870s

1889

Helen Beatrix Potter grew up in London, England, in a wealthy, artistic Victorian family. She was taught at home, and spent a lot of time reading and drawing. During long summer vacations, Beatrix and her brother, Bertram, roamed the countryside, collecting frogs, lizards, mice, and other creatures to sketch. Some were even smuggled home as pets! As an adult, Beatrix began selling her illustrations. She spent hours at London's Natural History Museum, studying and sketching plants and insects, and even went on to write a scientific paper about fungi. When she was twenty-seven, she sent a story based on her real-life pet rabbit, Peter Piper, to cheer up the unwell son of a friend. In other letters, she wrote stories about a fishing frog, and a rude squirrel named Nutkin. Years later, Beatrix decided to turn

c. 1890s

c. 1900s

the story of Peter the rabbit into a little book and paid for a small number of copies to be made. *The Tale of Peter Rabbit* became so popular that many more copies were printed, and it went on to become one of the most loved children's stories of all time. Beatrix wrote another twenty-two tales, some based on her actual pets, including a bunny called Benjamin and a hedgehog named Mrs. Tiggy-Winkle. In 1905, she bought Hill Top, a farm in the Lake District in the UK. She married a man named William Heelis, and threw herself into farming and raising sheep. After her death in 1943, she gave fifteen farms and over 4,000 acres of land to the UK-based conservation charity the National Trust, in the hope that the beautiful countryside she loved would stay protected.

Want to find out more about **Beatrix Potter**?

Have a read of this great book:

V&A Introduces: Beatrix Potter

If you visit the UK, you can visit Hill Top, which is protected by the National Trust.

To dear Delilah, dream big. The world awaits!

First published in the US in 2026 by Frances Lincoln Children's Books, an imprint of The Quarto Group.
Quarto Boston North Shore, 100 Cummings Center, Suite 265D, Beverly, MA 01915, USA
Tel: +1 978-282-9590 **www.Quarto.com**
EEA Representation, WTS Tax d.o.o., Žanova ulica 3, 4000 Kranj, Slovenia. www.wts-tax.si

ISBN 978-1-80570-163-7
Set in Futura BT.

Published by Juliet Matthews · Edited by Lucy Menzies
Editorial management by Izzie Hewitt
Designed by Sasha Moxon, Izzy Bowman, and Karissa Santos
Production by Robin Boothroyd
Manufactured in Shanghai, China CC102025
1 3 5 7 9 8 6 4 2

Photographic acknowledgements (pages 28-29, from left to right): 1. An undated library file picture of a young Beatrix Potter, age nine. 2. 1889: English writer Beatrix Potter. (Photo by Hulton Archive/Getty Images) 3. Portrait of British children's author Beatrix Potter, 1890s. (Photo by Express Newspapers/Getty Images) 4. Beatrix Potter by King—Image ID: JW69J6 (RM).

Collect the *Little People,* **BIG DREAMS**™ series:

FRIDA KAHLO, COCO CHANEL, MAYA ANGELOU, AMELIA EARHART, AGATHA CHRISTIE, MARIE CURIE, ROSA PARKS, AUDREY HEPBURN, EMMELINE PANKHURST

ELLA FITZGERALD, ADA LOVELACE, JANE AUSTEN, GEORGIA O'KEEFFE, HARRIET TUBMAN, ANNE FRANK, MOTHER TERESA, JOSEPHINE BAKER, L. M. MONTGOMERY

JANE GOODALL, SIMONE DE BEAUVOIR, MUHAMMAD ALI, STEPHEN HAWKING, MARIA MONTESSORI, VIVIENNE WESTWOOD, MAHATMA GANDHI, DAVID BOWIE, WILMA RUDOLPH

DOLLY PARTON, BRUCE LEE, RUDOLF NUREYEV, ZAHA HADID, MARY SHELLEY, MARTIN LUTHER KING JR., DAVID ATTENBOROUGH, ASTRID LINDGREN, EVONNE GOOLAGONG

BOB DYLAN, ALAN TURING, BILLIE JEAN KING, GRETA THUNBERG, JESSE OWENS, JEAN-MICHEL BASQUIAT, ARETHA FRANKLIN, CORAZON AQUINO, PELÉ

ERNEST SHACKLETON, STEVE JOBS, AYRTON SENNA, LOUISE BOURGEOIS, ELTON JOHN, JOHN LENNON, PRINCE, CHARLES DARWIN, CAPTAIN TOM MOORE

HANS CHRISTIAN ANDERSEN, STEVIE WONDER, MEGAN RAPINOE, MARY ANNING, MALALA YOUSAFZAI, ANDY WARHOL, RUPAUL, MICHELLE OBAMA, MINDY KALING

IRIS APFEL, ROSALIND FRANKLIN, RUTH BADER GINSBURG, MARILYN MONROE, KAMALA HARRIS, ALBERT EINSTEIN, CHARLES DICKENS, YOKO ONO, MICHAEL JORDAN

Scan the QR code for free activity sheets, teachers' notes and more information about the series at www.littlepeoplebigdreams.com